How to Organize Your Home

De-stress, Declutter and Organize Your Life

Using Simple and Effective Productivity

Techniques

By

Emily Jenkins

ISBN-13: 978-1727850772

ISBN-10: 1727850777

INTRODUCTION

We all crave to have organized homes. This is consequent upon the negative image that clutter has acquired. But much more than that, there is a sense of accomplishment that an organized home brings and people who have organized homes look forward to going back to it. An organized space has the capacity to reduce stress. The opposite is the case when one encounters a space filled with clutter. We become instinctively stressed without knowing exactly why.

This "need" to be organized however collides with our need to acquire items and our attachment to our possessions. As a result, it becomes difficult to organize your home when it is full of things, most of which you do not need.

Even the most organized people will find clutter crawling into their lives as soon as they begin to have kids. To make your organizing efforts yield any results, you must make it a family affair. Involve your kids and everyone else. Chances are, the kids will love the fact that they are involved in deciding where their things stay and will begin to organize their rooms on their own.

In the same vein, organizing your home becomes easier with practice. This is not to say you will not have to think about clutter. Clutter happens naturally as you try to keep track of all the things you have to do. It is the byproduct of a busy life. Clutter can creep into all aspects of our lives. It is not merely physical. You can have clutter all around you in the form of appointments to keep, a stuffed-up calendar, a mail box overflowing with documents to open and thousands of unread messages as well as a mental to-do list that you carry around and makes you feel overwhelmed. If you must de-stress and organize your life and not just your home, you must deal with all these kinds of clutter. Decluttering appropriately can increase your productivity.

However, most people view getting organized

as a daunting task. But it is not at all. It is daunting only at the start and is not always as overwhelming as it appears once you begin the process. Home organization is something that we can quickly adapt to. It does not have to be tasking. It does not have to sap your energy. It does not have to take all your time either. You can transform your home from one filled with clutter to one that is physically attractive by tackling clutter with proven methods. All of these can be achieved in a relatively short time. In this book, we have simplified the process of organizing your home and your life so that you are able to carry out your organizing with ease while following the guide we have provided. We have also touched on all the forms that clutter could take and what you can do about it. In certain cases, clutter may have nothing to do with arranging your home at all. They affect your life and your productivity thus making decluttering an all-round issue.

You will learn how to take out the stress by taking out the clutter. In the last chapter, we have dedicated a section to the principles of essentialism. A very thoughtful process of dealing with the root of clutter itself by taking on less. Your life will be less cluttered if you take on only the things you can handle. You will also learn through this book that you must not own everything within your reach before you can live a fulfilled life. In the end, you will see that a decluttered home and life brings enormous advantages and stress free living for you.

CHAPTER ONE

HOME ORGANIZING TRENDS IN THE 21ST CENTURY

Home organization has always been trendy but unlike what we have today, it was ruled by an 'out of sight, out of mind' mentality. With this approach, all it took to be organized was to tuck clutter away from prying eyes. This was easy with the products that the rubber tote industry had to offer. We just had to tuck our shoes and everything else we had into 'plastic pockets' behind the closet door or underneath the bed. We then leave things we considered gorgeous for everyone to see. As long as our extra possessions were hidden away, we were organized.

But this approach was to change because even though hidden storage was important, it was instrumental to building clutter by helping us forget the things we own. As a result, home organization has taken a new direction and Sue Pail, CEO of Closet Factory even describes it as getting more sophisticated. This sophistication is evidenced by the renewed interests of homeowners and prospective homeowners in organized space.

Thus, new homeowners are looking out for storage features that fit the decor of their home. They are concerned about how their things will be neatly stored. They want the details of their new homes designed in a way that the things they use everyday can be easy to organize. These trends resonate with the fact that an organized home rids its occupants of stress, saves them time and money and generally keeps their lives running smoothly.

Perhaps, this is also why the interior design industry has taken over publishing waves in recent years. New concepts have evolved in home organization at a fast growing pace. These trends have gotten our consumerist society actively interested because they portend a much better way to stay organized.

Some of them began as an exposition of cultural practices from foreign countries while others were personal inclinations to home organization. Be that as it may, we have been fully invested in all of these trends and we have watched newer ones take over older ones.

All the while, we seek better ways and better ideas to help us lead organized lives. It would seem therefore that home organization is the fulcrum of the 21st century. It opens us up to the abundance we seek by freeing up the space for it to occupy. It is a tide that we all should follow. Organizing your home is simply trendy in this century and this makes it deserving of attention. But some people are overwhelmed by it and do not know where to start. They simply have so many options.

Sue Pail has advised that 'we should not let our space become a source of stress, but rather a source of pride and excitement.' Although the interior design industry has simplified home organization by providing all you will need to help you get organized such as custom designed storage, bedroom cabinets, bins, trays, baskets and so on, you will need to inculcate habits that support your new lifestyle. A habit such as giving can help you get rid of excess items while affording you the joy of seeing those things become useful to someone else. You will need to develop life enhancing behavior that helps you keep clutter at bay. Purge your closets and storage regularly and give it all away or sell the items if you prefer. The new home organizing trends entreat you to think on a long term basis so that you inculcate efforts that are sustainable for you.

In the long run though, the system you choose to put in place for organizing your home is up to you. This system depends on how you want your home to look. So, go ahead and imagine your ideal home and then strive to achieve that. We will now consider a few of the concepts that has evolved in home organization lately.

MINIMALISM

Minimalism is a concept seeking to change the role of possessions in our lives. It simply means owning less. It is a practice suggesting that we redirect our attention from the things we own to life itself. Minimalists are of the opinion that we attach too much meaning to our material possessions and in the process, we forsake our health, our purpose, our relationships and our desire to add value to the world. We redirect our focus from all these beautiful things to the objects that we own.

Minimalism is about finding real freedom from the claws of our material possessions so that we can live our best life. Minimalism proposes that we own less but then if we must own a lot, the idea of minimalism enables us to make that decision more consciously and more deliberately. You can choose to have fifteen cars but this should be a conscious decision and not one that is keeping you away from attaining your full potential. Your "stuff" can draw you back simply by holding all of your attention. This is what minimalism aims to curb. Minimalism is therefore a tool that can assist us in 'finding freedom from the trappings of the consumer culture we have built our lives around'. It is 'a tool to rid yourself of life's excess in favor of focusing on what's important - so you can find happiness, fulfilment and freedom.'

Therefore, minimalism helps us to find real happiness, one that is not tied to the things we own but tied to life itself.

Notable minimalists include Leo Babauta, Joshua Becker, Colin Wright who owns fifty-one things and travels the world, and Tammy Strobel. All these people are minimalists and as a result have been able to lead purpose driven lives.

KONMARI

Konmari is a Japanese home organization concept that was brought to life by Marie Kondo in her best-selling book, **The Life-Changing Magic of Tidying Up**. In this book, she outlined her personal method of organizing. The konmari method attaches decluttering to organization and it proposes that you tidy up your things in a way that you hold on to only possessions that are useful to you. Although the trait of usefulness is evidenced by the ability that these things possess to spark joy for you. Thus, keep only the things that make you happy. Every other thing, you should do away with. The konmari method suggests that you should fill your home with things that bring you joy. It also suggests that creating order is simple and you cannot get rid of clutter by transferring it somewhere else. To truly practice konmari, you must show gratitude for the things you own.

Konmari is practiced by picking your items one

after the other and considering whether they bring you joy. If they do, you can keep them but if they do not, you can toss them out. Your decision to keep or remove your items will therefore be based on your reactions to them. The idea of what brings joy differs from person to person and objects can spark joy either based on their use or on the memory they represent. A blender could be worthless until you think of the stress it rids you of when you attempt to cook. A birthday card could be ordinarily useless because it is old but it could spark joy when you think about who you received it from. Konmari is a mindful way to declutter and to keep only things that are of sentimental value to you.

HYGGE

Hygge is an extension of konmari and is the mindfulness concept that succeeds it. Hygge continues where konmari stops and proposes that our things not only spark joy but also makes our lives cozy. Hygge is a Danish word translated as 'cozy'. The term Hygge is difficult to explain but it is a way of living that surrounds you with happiness, warmth, love and lots of comfort. Practicing Hygge entails inculcating lots of activities into your life that makes your life not only meaningful but also enjoyable. Living Hygge is anticipating and living out the next big adventure. TIME magazine has explained Hygge in an article to broadly mean "an approach to living that embraces positivity and enjoyment of everyday experiences, said to be core concepts of attitudes to life in the Nordic region."

Hygge is used to describe feelings or moments that you consider cozy or special. It does not align to a set of rules and there is no specific way to practice Hygge. The only thing that Hygge requires of you is your consciousness or your mindfulness in the moment.

Perhaps, the best description given to Hygge is that penned by Helen Russell, author of **The Year of Living Danishly.** She says it is a "complete absence of anything annoying or emotionally overwhelming,' with 'a focus on togetherness and prioritizing the people in your life."

Thus, Hygge is a way of life that the Danes have put together to make life easier to live. It has been reported that they put the concept together "because they were trying to survive boredom, cold, dark and sameness" and that it has been around for centuries. Through practicing Hygge, the Danes have been able to find moments to celebrate. Activities that constitute Hygge are usually simple rituals that end up making the day special. These rituals could range from brewing a cup of tea to lighting a candle. They see life as art and as such feel that we can create the moments that make us feel 'cozy' ourselves. Hygge for us today could include looking at the smile of a partner or tucking our little finger into the folded palm of a crying baby. It could be hanging out with friends or picking up flowers for our lover. Whatever our Hygge ritual, we incorporate it into our lives by making time for it. Louisa Thompson, author of **Book of Hygge** describes it as 'finding that which brings you closeness and wraps you up in its embrace'.

Hygge is a reminder of something we already know. The fact that we should do things that make us happy. This is different from doing things that you feel obligated to do and so is essential to organizing your life and removing stress from it. Finding joy and being present can even help you clear your mental space. Therefore, Hygge is essential to your mental health. When it comes to decluttering, Hygge requires that we find coziness in our personal effects. We should enjoy them. While konmari theorizes that we should tuck some of our things in our closet to attain an organized home, Hygge leans more on displaying them if they will help us achieve joyful moments. Thus, stepping into your house and seeing that lovely picture of your spouse could produce the Hygge feeling for you and make you Hyggeligt.

DOSTADNING

Dostadning is a Swedish word that is translated

to mean 'death cleaning'. Do means death and stadning means cleaning. It is based on Swedish culture and is a home organization concept that proposes that we organize our possessions before death arrives. Death cleaning means that we should shred our possessions and neatly arrange all that is left in such a way that they do not become a burden to our loved ones when we pass away. Although, death cleaning targets the elderly, it can be done at any age and its principles can be used to organize your home even though you are not thinking about death.

Dostadning was popularized by the Swedish artist, Margareta Magnusson in her book **The Gentle Art of Swedish Death Cleaning: How**

to Free Yourself and Your Family from a Lifetime of Clutter. The death cleaning phenomenon has grown very popular thereby overshadowing the other home organization trends. More importantly, it has pushed people to act on the mass of possessions in their homes. It has opened up discussions about death in families and it has made inheritance easy as people can get what they truly want from an elderly loved one while he or she is still alive rather than resigning to whatever they are given at the loved one's death.

Dostadning emphasizes giving and explains that it is joyful to see your things being put to use while you are still alive. It also warns that if you do not give all your things a purpose while you still can, they might end up at an auction and worse still may not mean anything to anyone. The principles of dostadning are exact in nature, telling you what to do with what.

The Swedish decluttering concept is practiced by going through your possessions and sorting them yourself. You have your loved ones over while you do this. You then pick each item and evaluate it asking yourself if it would make anyone happier to keep it. If you answer this question in the affirmative, you then keep the item. If you answer in the negative, you toss it away. Also, you ask your loved ones which of your things they want and you give these to them.

Offer the rest of your things as presents and as donations. Keep the things that mean a lot to you alone in a throw away box and relish them while you are still alive. Your loved ones will know to throw these out once you pass away. For all the other things that have no usefulness, you can simply toss. This way, you will leave an organized home behind. Since the timing of death is unknown, you can live much longer than when you began to death clean. As a result, death cleaning never ends. Or to put it better, it ends at death. It is a continuous process and something you should keep at to ensure that clutter does not accumulate again. The Swedes practice death cleaning three times a year using the cultural practice to declutter and purge their homes. Once you begin death cleaning, you must ensure that you do not rush out and begin buying items that you do not need all over again. This will only take you to where you started.

Death cleaning is hard work but its principles of giving and involving others make it fun and something that even young people can practice. It offers a complete guide on how to declutter each item you own, from your books to your pets. It also encompasses how to declutter your digital assets making it easy for your loved ones to access your digital accounts and financial institutions when you pass away. Dostadning as a home organization trend has decluttering at its heart and is most notable for not being directed at the person who is practicing it but at his or her loved ones. In this way, dostadning is a selfless act unlike minimalism, konmari or Hygge that are self-directed. Dostadning is simply an act of kindness to the next generation and a way to show your children and other survivors that you love them and you very much want to reduce the pain of their grief.

Dostadning in its Entirety

Death cleaning seems such an odd concept but in reality it is not. It is not a sad endeavor but one that is thoughtful and proactive. Survivors of people who did not death clean have told stories of the pain that they have been through sorting their beloved deceased's items. However, death cleaning extends beyond the items alone. It is an all-inclusive decluttering activity. Dostadning has three aspects as follows:

1. Physical death cleaning

2. Digital death cleaning; and

3. Financial death cleaning

Physical Death Cleaning

Physical death cleaning otherwise referred to as physical death management is the most popular form of death cleaning. It is the aspect that includes your physical house and your physical possessions. It is more relevant to us when we intend to go about organizing our home. It is the sort of death cleaning we are involved in when we sort through our items, determining their usefulness to us or to others and then decluttering them. It is the heart of dostadning. For physical death cleaning, the dostadning phenomenon does not want you to leave items behind that are a trouble to deal with. Also, these items that you leave behind should be as minimal as possible.

Digital Death Cleaning

This form of death cleaning speaks to our digital clutter. The world has gone digital and we are living in an age that cannot survive without the unique method of information exchange; the Internet. This tool is also a cause of the information overload that we experience. Because of our involvement in the tide, we have aspects of our lives that are entirely online. Dostadning proposes that when we are no longer on this planet, there should be a system in place that makes our on-line existence easy to deal with. Our survivors should not have a hard time going through our online information and deciding what to do with them.

The concept also provides practical ways to address this situation. It says that you should keep a book of passwords that is easy for your loved ones to locate. Put down your passwords. Do not leave your loved ones second guessing what those passwords are and don't count on their memory and ability to remember either. Specifically put it down so that they do not get stranded accessing this when you are no longer around. However, digital death cleaning is taking a new dimension and the trends are showing that digital death managers are likely to be on the upsurge soon. These digital death managers will of course be professionals saddled with managing the digital life of a deceased person. Your duty as dostadning posits is to make your digital content easy to access for your survivors.

Financial Death Cleaning

An important aspect of dostadning is financial

death cleaning. This is more or less death cleaning your finances. Dostadning suggests that you make the money you leave behind in your financial institutions easy to access. Our financial institutions go beyond the physical banks. Some of us have online bank accounts. When you pass away, your loved ones will be unable to access these accounts if you have not set up a system for them to. If they do not know the pins of your debit cards and credit cards, they will have to go through arduous processes to access your finances. To death clean these types of possessions appropriately, you will need to keep a book that holds your login information for all your financial institutions. This way, your loved ones will have an easier ride accessing your money at the bank.

Together, minimalism, konmari, hyyge, dostadning along with a host of other unpopular concepts point to one truth: organizing your home is incredibly important. It is significant to your wellbeing and the wellbeing of others as dostadning suggests. It reduces stress and makes your life run smoothly. But all these concepts emphasize that you organize not only your home but also your life in the form of finding and keeping things that spark joy for you or make you Hyggeligt and in the form of directing your attention from your possessions to your purpose and your ability to contribute beyond yourself.

Also, you must organize your home and consequently your life in the process of dostadning in such a way that it makes your life run with ease and also puts a smile on your loved one's faces while you are still living and when you pass away. These concepts have taken mindfulness to a whole new level in this century at a time when we truly need it as technological upsurge has directed our attention from ourselves and from people to things. However, the home organization method you choose is up to you, whether it is one that helps you keep your home in order now or one that helps you reflect on life as well.

CHAPTER TWO

WHAT IS DECLUTTERING ABOUT AND WHY IS IT SO IMPORTANT?

Decluttering is the new way out of a hectic life. Our lives can get so busy and demanding; juggling between kids, jobs and house chores. It can get to a point when we really do need a break. Things begin to pile up and when we look at all the things we need to do; we begin to wonder how they piled up in the first place. Our dishwasher never seems to dry up and the laundry room is ever sprawling with loads of laundry to be done. Most of us escape from it all by thinking that when we have our homes redone, everything will be fine. But the truth is that the pattern will only continue if we do not have a system in place to keep the ever building pile of work in check.

We need to automatically minimize the things calling for our attention. The concept is so important that there is a national body targeted at it. The Institute for Challenging Disorganization (ICD) formerly called the National Study Group on Chronic Disorganization are busy professionals combatting clutter. The Institute is a non-profit organization aimed at helping people who are organizationally challenged. This goes to show how important decluttering is.

Decluttering is simply getting rid of clutter. It

can take many forms such as shredding your possessions and giving it all away to maintaining a highly organized home, one that does not look like a mess. All the concepts we talked about in chapter one points to one method of decluttering or the other. The crux of decluttering is organizing your possessions in such a way that your house does not look like that of a hoarder and if it does look that way then at least things should be properly arranged and not look upsetting. Tackling clutter is not easy because it builds up really fast and can get out of control but then it is not a chore that we can avoid. You can begin decluttering by considering why you should get involved with it at all.

IMPORTANCE OF DECLUTTERING

The first step to achieving your decluttering goal is understanding its personal importance to you. Thus, decluttering because someone asked you to or because someone nagged you into it is not going to get you anywhere. Consider why an organized home is important to you or what you stand to gain from getting organized. Having personal decluttering goals will set you up for the long run and enable you adopt and maintain an organization system that you can sustain. Write down ways that decluttering can benefit you. Whether it is your home or your office that needs to be organized. Write down in your journal, five ways that decluttering these places can make your life better in the long run.

These are your decluttering goals and you should keep them somewhere you can easily access them as a reminder of why you need to declutter and get organized in the process. Decluttering is both physically, emotionally and mentally beneficial to you. It has been said that a cluttered mind causes you to be restless and unfocused. It clouds your vision and adds stress to your life. In fact, studies have shown that all the clutter around you can affect your concentration and the ability of your brain to process information. Neuroscientists at Princeton University have detected a relationship between decrease in performance and an increase in stress levels to physical clutter.

When you have a lot of things to do, clutter in your surrounding can compete for your attention thereby lowering your likelihood of proper execution. Research has also linked changes in mood and a decreased self-esteem to clutter.

When the UCLA's Center on Everyday Lives and Families (CELF) undertook this study, they found that the amount of stress that 82 families who were subject of the research experienced was directly proportional to the amount of objects in their home. This goes to show that decluttering leads to a sharpened mind and helps with better focus. In the long run, decluttering enables you to achieve goals that are important to you by opening you up to a better life.

Decluttering your surroundings also serves your emotional needs because most of your possessions are of sentimental value to you. When you throw out a journal filled with angry memories of an ex for example, you will find that you think of them less and that such action is a foundation for forgetting all the bad memories associated with that person. So, decluttering serves you emotionally, physically and mentally.

We will consider more benefits of decluttering

when we begin to talk about clutter itself.

HOW CLUTTER ACCUMULATES

One proactive definition of clutter is that it is procrastination in its physical form. Another definition is that it is anything we do not 'need or use that saps our time, energy and space.' Clutter is all those things that we have cramped together in our home. It is the dirty dishes in the dishwasher that just won't go away. It is the overflowing laundry and the messy floors. It is the clothes tucked behind the closet that you have forgotten that you own. Clutter is everything that represents disorganization and that manifests itself before we get enough time to breathe. Clutter is synonymous with disorder as it makes you lose things, makes it difficult for you to find things and consequently makes you acquire more and spend more. Each time you cannot find those set of sneakers, you just rush out and get another to enable you get on with your activities as planned. Even though we can easily spot clutter in the house of someone who is a hoarder, clutter is much more than that because a hoarder might not have clutter in his environment if he has a large enough space to contain it.

Thus, clutter is mostly present when you accumulate more possessions than you have space to contain. The contents of a cramped one-bedroom apartment may therefore not be clutter if they are transferred into a duplex. Clutter distorts your perception of home and your feelings of satisfaction with life. This was the finding of some researchers at the University of New Mexico in 2016. But how do we get to that state? **How exactly does clutter accumulate?**

Clutter happens unconsciously although it is a direct result of our conscious acts. It accumulates as we continually acquire new things. It is not the acquisition itself that causes clutter but our attachment to things. For some reason, even though we no longer use an item, we often choose not to let it go. We hold on to it and end up with clutter. Sometimes, it is because of the money we have spent on it but other times, it is because of some other emotion we may have attached to it. Hence, our homes become full of things that we have not touched at all and some of which we have totally forgotten about. Clutter then builds up making our space look unorganized. Sometimes, these things are just "bad buys". Things we made mistakes buying or things that simply do not fit our style. They could even be things that were once okay but are no longer trendy. Letting go of things that we have become attached to simply causes us pain. Researchers at Yale University have proven that our brains view the loss of a possession that we attach value to as a loss that is capable of causing physical pain. This is why it is so hard to declutter.

We are emotionally attached to our possessions, and this emotional attachment makes us hold on to them even when we no longer need them. The result is clutter and this is not healthy either as clutter causes distress and makes our brain unable to focus and process information. Thus, a cluttered environment negatively impacts your brain, your performance and your productivity. This is why you will be better off experiencing the momentary pain associated with letting go of things that you no longer use.

Types of Clutter

Clutter extends beyond a desk full of papers or things that you can physically move around. Clutter can be present in all aspects of our lives. There are four types of clutter as follows:

1. Physical clutter

2. Mental clutter

3. Emotional clutter; and

4. Digital clutter

Physical Clutter

Physical clutter is the accumulation and disorganization that is visible all around you. Things you can see and touch. Physical clutter refers to your physical possessions. The ones that get you worried when they are lumped together all around your house. Things like books, clothes, plates and so on.

Mental Clutter

This is the kind of clutter your brain experiences when it is faced with your physical clutter. It becomes a sort of psychic baggage and impedes your performance as it fights for your attention and consequently your focus. This baggage arises because of a lack of clarification. Your brain does not understand why the physical environment is so full of things that appear disorganized. Your memory never lets go of the scene and it allows it to clog your mind. Mental clutter affects us in profound ways. A study at University of Toronto by Lynn Hasher has pointed out mental clutter as a cause of age related memory losses.

Emotional Clutter

Emotional clutter is the natural byproduct of our negative experiences. 'Everyone has emotional clutter'. Emotional clutter accumulates as we encounter challenges, disappointment, failures and rejection. We feel pain and then store the pain as the residue of the experience. Emotional clutter evidences itself in the frustration that we feel from time to time when we encounter situations that remind us of the ones that hurt us in the past. The easiest way to release emotional clutter is by practising forgiveness. Letting go of the past and focusing on the present. Recognize the emotional baggage and declutter it. This is the only way to prevent it from disguising new opportunities as ultimate failures.

Digital Clutter

Digital clutter as the name implies is clutter that comes from a digital source. It is more or less technological clutter. The kind of clutter that technological advancement has brought our way. They are clutter because they take up space and impede our productivity. They prevent us from focusing on the things that are most important to us. Digital clutter includes notifications from your social media accounts like Facebook and Twitter, your unread messages in your mail box, files scattered all around your computer, or even information constantly coming your way. The overconsumption of digital data has the same effect on our brains as physical clutter. Digital clutter often takes the form of information coming at us at a rate faster than what we can take.

Disadvantages of Clutter

It is obvious from the previous discussions that clutter carries significantly negative repercussions. Clutter has been described as being both a symptom and a cause of stress and carrying the capacity to disrupt every area of your life. It is a distraction that drags us back more than we want it. Having said this, let us take a look at specific disadvantages of allowing clutter creep into our lives.

1. Stress

Clutter increases our anxiety levels as cortisol which is the stress hormone responds in skyrocketing levels to cluttered environments.

2. Time wastage

Clutter results in enormous waste of time. The time it takes you to look for items in a cluttered environment is better used on something else. When we allow the dishwasher fill up unattended to, we spend much more time attending to it than we would have spent initially.

3. Clutter deteriorates your mental health

Researchers at University of South Carolina proved that clutter negatively affects mental health. The study found that a comfortable environment was essential to optimal mental health. Thus, a cluttered environment can diminish work place satisfaction and the mental condition of the employees. The situation is invariably the same for clutter experienced at home.

4. Inability to identify with your home

People who have cluttered homes may find it hard to see it as a place to get relief from the pressure they experience in the outside world. The cluttered home environment merely adds to this mental torture. Clutter has therefore been shown to be capable of affecting our psychological sense of home.

5. Clutter impedes our thinking

Clutter in the mind can make our thinking less efficient. We become slower at processing information and less effective at multitasking because we are unable to think at an efficient pace.

Clutter accumulates because we attach meaning to our possessions and see them as an extension of ourselves. We also see our homes as an extension of ourselves and we want to define our space by fitting it with our possessions. It is when it becomes excessive that the clutter problem develops, this is called the clutter effect. It then threatens us physically and 'psychologically entraps a person in dysfunctional home environments which contributes to personal distress and feelings of displacement and alienation'. Tackling clutter is therefore something you should set aside time to achieve.

CHAPTER THREE

STEP-BY-STEP GUIDE TO DECLUTTERING YOUR LIVING SPACE

Once you have decided to get rid of the clutter in your home, your first concern will be its paralyzing effect. Facing the clutter can make you abandon it and do nothing about it because you may be uncertain about where and how to start. For this reason, you need to set up a plan for decluttering your home.

You need a step by step guide to help you overcome clutter and it is essential that this guide is one that is sustainable. We will take you through how to organize your home reaching to every nook and cranny of your house in this chapter.

The Golden Rule of Home Organization

First, you must know and conform to the golden rule of organizing. This rule says that inventory must conform to storage. Thus, you must begin your decluttering from your storage spaces. Empty out the drawers, the shelfs and the cabinets so that after you have taken stock of what to keep, you will be able to decide where to keep them.

The 3 Rs of Oganization

There are three guiding principles of home

organization otherwise known as the three Rs. They are reduction, resourcefulness and resilience. Decluttering in the form of reducing what you have is the first step to organizing. Being resourceful requires that you find ways to use the few things that you have and make them more useful. The third R, resilience speaks to the fact that if you do not have something, you should make do with what you have.

Attach a Cause to Your Organizational Goals

The guilt that comes with decluttering sentimental items and the hard work that decluttering and organizing carry in general will be eliminated if you are organizing for a worthy cause. This way also, somebody else will be benefiting from your organizing efforts. Donate your items that you will be taking out and gain an organized home in return. You would have put a smile on people's faces in the process.

Group Like Items Together

While you are organizing, put items that are similar together so that they are easy to locate when you need them. Toothbrushes can stay together for example and so can cooking utensils. Organize your home in such a way that drawers, shelfs and cabinets have the specific items they carry. When you sort out a drawer, you know exactly what is in it and you are not faced with a random combination of items.

Don't Try to do Everything At the Same Time

Chances are clutter is keeping you from being able to multitask effectively anyway, so stop it. Try to pick projects one at a time. When you want to go about organizing your home, don't start at multiple places. This will leave you exhausted. When organizing a room, don't go on to new drawers when you have not finished the ones you have started decluttering. If you multitask or arrange your items haphazardly, you will end up tired without having achieved your goals.

Use Up Every Space Available

If your family is still growing, then it might be

really difficult to find space to keep things. This can be the case even after you have decluttered. You may end up with more things than you have the space to keep. The way out of this situation is to use up every space available such as on top of the refrigerator. Keep items that you do not use often out of the cabinets that you use often but make sure to find the next available space for them.

Reinvent Your Landing Strip

Make your landing strip more effective. Add more hooks and more items but make sure each item has a purpose so that it does not add to the clutter. Umbrella, keys, shoes and all kinds of things end up here. For example, Shoes can be kept in a basket by the door.

Possession Self-Extension

This simply means seeing things as an extension of yourself. This is why you hold on to them and find it difficult to let them go. But you must get rid of those that only add to the clutter in your home. To effectively achieve this, you must consider and redefine your relationship with your belongings. Be their owner and do not let them own you.

Now let's take a physical tour of your house and begin getting it organized.

TAKE IT ONE ROOM AT A TIME

It is essential that you begin organizing from one spot in your house, not from multiple spots if you intend to achieve anything. So, take your home organization one room at a time.

1. Floors are supposed to be empty

Pick up clothes from the floor and enforce a rule that makes it stay that way. Having clothes scattered all over and on the floor will do nothing to help your tidying up. Go about with a large basket to pick up anything that will be going out.

2. Keep flat surfaces clear

Flat surfaces include tables, shelves, dressers, nightstands and so on. Remove anything you have on top of these. Make the bed and clear out anything on the nightstand. Keep only the things you will need by bedtime on the nightstand. You can keep a lamp, a pen, a journal and a book on the nightstand but nothing more. This way it will look organized. For other flat surfaces, keep their tops bare.

3. Sort the items

As you go from room to room, make sure to sort out the items. Decide which ones you need and which ones you do not need. Decide what to do with what you do not need, whether to toss them out or to donate them.

4. Clear out drawers and fill them again

The trick to organizing like we have said before is to empty out your storage areas before refilling them again. Clear out your drawers, closets, etc. and then place back in an organized manner, things that you have decided to keep. Arrange the storage areas back in such a way that things are not hidden away but everything is within view.

5. Do not leave any storage area out

As you open cabinets, drawers, bags and so on, do not leave them halfway and move on to others. Finish sorting out their contents before moving on. Look over at the drawer you just finished organizing and find encouragement in the fact that the next one will look that good when you are done with it.

6. Consider your shoes

Like clothes, shoes can easily get out of hand.

We can have so much more of them than we need. You can use shoe boxes to keep your shoes out of sight or organized. You can also choose to limit the number of shoes you own by keeping just enough to cater for your shoe needs. You can organize this into the back of your closet or you can dedicate one row in your closet to your shoes.

The Sitting Room

This is the most often used as well as most cluttered room in the house. The sitting room can easily get filled up with children's toys, DVDs and board games. This could be a really tough room to organize as a result of the amount of traffic (objects and people) that pass through. To take care of this room, you have to take it in stages. Start from the parts of the room that you are most worried about. You can also set up a system to visually divide up the room. Create a play area that contains the kids' toys and let them know that they cannot exceed this space. Arrange everything else into their appropriate place and take out anything else that does not belong in this room. For the wires and cables, you can use a cable management sleeve to wrap them up or you can pass them through a pipe out of your house.

Kids' Bedroom

This room is usually a mess although not in the eyes of its occupants. Tackle these room by creating a space for toys as you did in the sitting room. Pick clothes off the floor and the bed and arrange the closet. The most effective organizing tip for this room is getting those little hands to do it with you. Ask them where they want things to be and place the items there if their suggestions work for you too. Enforce discipline to keep clutter from reoccurring here.

Bathrooms

Bathrooms can get easily messy. You could have pottys, towels, soaps and brushes lying in every corner and dirt can easily crawl onto the surfaces of objects in this room. The easiest way to organize the bathroom is to clean everything in it scrubbing and washing as you go. Bring out all the clean items and attend to the walls, the bathtubs and showers, etc. When the bathroom looks sparkling, you can then bring in all the items and place them where you want them to be. Throw out items that are no longer of any use, like finished toothpastes, bathing lotions, shampoos, etc. You can also get a small shelf that you hang up and store the products.

Pay Attention to Your Closet

The closet is often one of the most challenging things to organize. This is because of how easy it is for thing to get piled up. We do this unconsciously by first starting to hide things away in it. We believe that our room is organized once the clutter is hidden away behind the closet door. But this is usually not the case. We end up with clutter behind that door that we will soon have to face. To organize your closet, remove everything in it and clean it. Sort out the items you removed and begin replacing only those you want to keep.

While standing in front of your closet, decide where each item will go. Like shoes in the back row etc. It is helpful to keep only items that you love and that you will use or already use frequently. You can toss out or donate items that you have not worn in the last six months or you can make decluttering your closet much more fun by shopping in it. Take out those clothes you have not worn for a long time and try them out in front of the mirror deciding which ones you will like to start wearing all over again. Any clothes or other items that do not enter your 'begin using' list should be on their way out of your house.

What About the Laundry?

The laundry room can also get very messy. The room is perfect for hiding away dirt and overflowing clothes that need washing. This is why you need to pay attention to your laundry room when you are organizing your home. Use glass jars to hold laundry supplies like detergent so it is easy to see when they are getting used up and there should be no excuse for missing laundry days. Take advantage of equipment that allow your laundry room to be easy to use such as ones with open shelving and inbuilt supports for folding clothes and sorting them out. The easiest tip to help you with your laundry however is to limit them. Don't allow the dirty clothes to pile up. Set up a routine that allows you to deal with them from time to time. Don't exhaust yourself however by dealing with your laundry in bits such as on a daily basis. This is not good for your long term goals of de-stressing.

Declutter Your Kitchen

The kitchen tells its own story of clutter, from the food stains on the counter to the crumbs on the floor. There is no doubt that this is a frequently used room. You must begin organizing this room by taking inventory of all that is in it. You will find that you have lots of excess items here. Items that you do not use and some you may never get to use. Eliminate these items. Clean out your cabinets before filling them up again. Place the garbage can where you can easily access it to toss unwanted items into it. Get rid of plates, bowls, utensils, and trays that no longer serve you.

Clear out the dishwasher and keep it

unoccupied. Go through your spices and throw out any that are expired. A trick that can help you keep your kitchen clean is to place the garbage can where it can be easy to access. Instead of keeping it under the counter, bring it out into the open so that your family gets to use it rather than throwing trash on the floor. Keep countertops clear and organized and let surfaces appear squeaky clean.

Pay Attention to Your Home Office

Some of us work from home and even if you don't, you probably have an area of your house where you handle work related issues. If you do, you will need to take care of this space and get it working for you again.

Use the flat surfaces rule to tackle your table top. Clear out everything on top of your desk and in your drawers. Place all the items on the floor and clean the desk. Then, sort through the items to determine their usefulness and consequently their destination. Use a bin to hold all bills and receipts. Toss out items that have no place in this room before you deal with the rest.

For office supplies and stationaries, use the drawers. Arrange each project you are working on into a file and create an alphabetical filing system with files arranged on the floor in one corner of the room or on shelves. Allow your desk to lay bare or everything will get cluttered again. You can leave your phone and your computer on the desk. Each time you work, make sure you have only the documents you are working on at the time laying on top of your desk.

Decluttering Order for Your Living Space

It helps to have an order when you go about organizing your home. Start with storage spaces like your garage or hall closet then move on to shared spaces like the sitting room and the kitchen and finish up with personal spaces like your bedroom. Clearing out storage first allows you have a place to put things while you are decluttering.

CHAPTER FOUR

REDUCING STRESS AND INCREASING YOUR PRODUCTIVITY

Stress is detrimental to our health and general wellbeing. It can even impede our performance and affect our productivity. When you line up activities more than you can attend to, you will end up feeling pressured with deadlines to meet. We tend to arrange more tasks for ourselves than we can carry out. In order for you to be productive, you must be specific about how you are going to handle the stress that taking on too much pushes at you.

True productivity has been described as 'being

able to create, generate or bring new ideas, products or services to life.' If we could focus on only one task within a set amount of time and get it done, we would have been productive. We are mostly unproductive because we are very busy doing things that we do not love. We try to be productive on tasks that we do not enjoy. As a result, distractions creep in easily in the form of the ever present Internet and social media or in the form of getting on to a different task or starting conversations with people around us.

To reduce your stress and increase productivity, you must direct your efforts at this goal mindfully. We have distilled some ways through which you can achieve this below.

1. Meditation

Meditation is a powerful way to de-stress. It directs the energy flowing in your day and relieves your negativity.

2. Set routines

When you do not set routines, you tackle tasks as they come or according to your moods. A to-do list and an established method of doing things enables you to achieve more. They give your day a direction and they ease your stress because you tackle tasks as you have predetermined and not haphazardly. It is advisable that you begin with the most difficult tasks so that you get those out of the way before going on to smaller tasks. You can also begin with tasks that have the earliest deadlines.

3. Combine tasks

By combine tasks, we mean that you lump them together. Doing a particular type of task each day when you can do it weekly or bi-weekly will impede your productivity. For example, do your laundry at weekends instead of everyday. This makes it a less stressful assignment and this way, it does not take up the time that you ought to spend doing other things.

4. Learn from your activities

Approaching your activities with an open mind that positions you to learn makes the task more enjoyable. Rather than performing your tasks grudgingly, be curious enough to seek what is new in the task.

5. Practice clarity

Clarity makes our objectives easier to achieve. Practice clarity by simplifying your decisions. Simply answer yes or no when you are trying to decide on whether to take on a new project. Chances are projects that you are skeptical about end up burdensome if you go about them anyway.

6. Always have a journal and a pen with you

Putting down things that we need to do places us one step ahead and enables us to achieve them. Each night or as you wrap up your work day, write down the things you need to achieve the next day. Then, arrange these items by their priority. This guides you through your tasks the next day, reduces the stress you would have encountered and makes you more productive.

7. Renew your focus

Approach your tasks with a renewed focus. Be specific about what exactly you want to achieve. Working aimlessly whether at home or at the office can increase your stress and decrease your productivity. When you are sure about the importance of a task at hand, you are able to perform it with vigor to a reasonable end.

Decluttering Physically and Mentally

In chapter three, we have gone through a practical method for decluttering physically. To adequately deal with clutter, you must take care of your mental clutter also.

If you are always going about with your mental to-do-list or you find yourself thinking about the past / being anxious about the future, then your mind is clogged with mental clutter. This type of clutter makes it impossible for you to concentrate. Your mind just keeps wandering and you are unable to get anything done. This type of clutter is usually the residue of physical clutter. This is why the vital first step to decluttering mentally is decluttering your physical environment. A disorganized environment makes you less proactive. In addition, physical clutter exhausts your brain because you continually think that your tasks are unending. Your brain interprets the things in your surroundings as more work to do. To declutter mentally therefore, you must begin by decluttering physically. Take care of your physical environment. This environment includes anywhere you spend your time. It could be your home, car, office or some other place.

The reason that decluttering physically and mentally is so intertwined is the attachment we have to our possessions that makes us view them as extensions of ourselves. So look into the future you want and remove all things that do not support its outlook.

A life lived without any plans is doomed to fail. Whether it's a more organized home or a more organized life you want, you must be clear about your goals, put them down and work towards them. In the same vein, you should take stock of what you have accomplished as this gives you perspective and lets you know whether you are making any progress at all.

Declutter Your Friendships

Our relationships can drain our energy if they are toxic. This is why decluttering your friendships is important to your decluttering goals. You cannot take a step in the right direction if you hold on to people who only add to your stress. Consider how each friend adds to your goals or your purpose and reduce involvement with them if they are only detrimental to your objectives. Surround yourself with people who build your support system and help you achieve your goals.

Let Go of Resentment

On the other end of mental clutter is emotional clutter and one which deserves mention. Emotional clutter is the sum total of the baggage that we have held on to. It manifests itself in resentment, malice and unforgiveness. It keeps us from gratefulness and all the virtues that allow good things to flow towards us. To properly de-stress, you must let go of resentment. Forgive those who have hurt you and release the space for abundance to enter your life.

Practice Prioritizing

Establish a routine that allows you prioritize your activities. Do things according to your list of which ones are most important. Lists have a way of giving your mind order. While you are at this, make sure to get rid of procrastination and fear. Procrastination does not serve you, neither does your fear of accomplishment. Procrastination just postpones your tasks to the next day and the next one after that. The result is that other tasks add to them and you end up with a cluttered mind because of the overwhelming nature of your piled up tasks.

SELF-ORGANIZATION TOOLS

Some of us need specific tools to combat clutter. We need the perfect equipment that can help us de-stress and get organized. While these tools might be different from person to person, there are a few that we all can use in common. The tool that you need will be typically dependent on your requirements but the self-organization tools below can help anyone get organized and get rid of stress once and for all.

1. Calendar

You can keep track of your appointments and social engagements with a calendar. Mark important dates on your calendar and visit it from time to time. You can choose to use a physical calendar or a digital one. Google calendar is a highly recommended tool to help you stay organized.

2. Journal and pen

A journal and a pen can do wonders for your organization. It could be a notepad or a pocket notebook. You can put down ideas in your journal for your next organizational goals so that you do not forget them. Taking your journal and pen everywhere is beneficial to realizing your objectives. All you have to do is put down that thought. Make sure that it is a size that can easily fit into your bag.

3. A habit list

Aside from your to do list, create a habit list. In

this list, keep a record of your actions and habits you would like to change.

4. Landing Strip

A landing strip next to the front door is very essential to your home organization goals. You can have a whole lot of things arranged there. Its like where everyone dumps everything once they get back home. You can use hooks, boxes, baskets and so on to set up your landing strip. As your kids get back from school, they can easily hang their backpacks on the hooks. A lot of people have found landing strips useful for attaining their organizational goals.

5. Junk drawer

The junk drawer is an essential organization tool. It is where you drop all the things that have no description. It could be a physical drawer for physical clutter or a digital junk drawer for mental and digital clutter. Use a visible drawer to drop things that do not have a specific place to stay like dead batteries, your products' manuals and so on. For the digital junk drawer, simply create an electronic page where you keep all the thoughts coming at you. You can create this page on your computer or in a journal. This will help you clear the space for other thoughts and you can also go back to the drawer when you need some inspiration.

6. Index Cards

Index cards can help you stay organized in the

way of slipping them out of your pocket or bag to get a quick look at your to-do-list. They are portable and easy to use. You can start using a stack of these cards for your self-organization.

7. The Trash Can

Otherwise called a garbage can. This self-organization tool helps keep your home organized by taking care of all sorts of dirt and unwanted items out of it.

There are many more self-organization tools of course but you can try these and you do not have to try them all at a time. Simply choose which ones work best for you.

DEALING WITH DIGITAL CLUTTER

Digital clutter is the clutter of the new age. The 21st century kind of clutter brought to us by technological advancement and by development itself. It is that clutter that keeps your phone beeping incessantly and sways your concentration every time. What can you do with this type of clutter?

To effectively declutter and organize your life, you must deal with digital clutter. Here are a few ways you can do that.

1. Set a limit on the information you receive

There are lots of outlets through which information reaches us in today's world. The information flowing towards us is endless and can get very overwhelming. Too much of information results in information clutter, a form of digital clutter, and has been said to be capable of clogging the brain. To deal with this, you must set limits on the information you receive. Choose which information you want to digest. You can do this by reducing your consumption. Limit the number of things you read both on social media and on your subscriptions. Unsubscribe from blogs, websites and magazines that provide mind-numbing data that add no real value to you. Limit your television time as well choosing carefully only programs that matter to you.

2. Declutter your mail box

An overflowing inbox can be very distracting.

As a rule, try not to read a mail twice before you determine its usefulness to you. Use the custom made organizing tips to mark some of your mail as important so that you can come back to them if you find that you need the information such mail contains. Unsubscribe from promotions or newsletters that never bring value to you. Turn off notifications from social media sites like Facebook, LinkedIn and Twitter. Separate your mail into the different sections provided in your inbox to minimize what you see immediately you log into your mail. There are numerous applications that you can use to control your mail if these work for you. You can also use other programs to schedule emails you intend to send and to set reminders.

3. Organize Your Computer

The desktop of your computer probably looks horrible as it is filled with files and folders in a haphazard manner. You might not need some of these files and there might be applications/icons on your computer that you no longer need as well. Decluttering digitally will involve you getting rid of these. Check for unused files regularly and remove them.

CHAPTER FIVE

KEEPING TRACK OF CLUTTER

Perhaps the most important step in home organization is keeping track of clutter. This is also true for organizing your life and de-stressing. You must be on top of the various forms of clutter making sure that they do not derail you in your plans of keeping your life and your home in order.

You must make sure that clutter does not resurface and take over your life.

The best way to achieve this is to maintain the system that you have put in place to combat clutter. Be clear about the level of organization you want to see in your home. Do you want to keep your things in a manner that makes them easy to spot? Do you want to know exactly where everything is located? You can achieve this by the system that you have put in place to tackle clutter. But it is more important for this system to be sustainable. It is more important that you maintain it. Be clear about how organized you want to be. Know what works for you because in the end, it is your definition of clutter that truly matters.

If photographs on the wall of your bedroom do not represent clutter for you then they are not. If they do for someone else in the way that they impede their productivity, then they are clutter for them. To keep track of clutter, you must be specific about what standards you want to attain.

To keep track of clutter, you must act fast to get rid of them as they begin to accumulate. Do not wait till the last minute when your energy is drained. A good example is leaving the plates in the dishwasher after every meal and then ending up too tired to deal with them which then makes you leave them till the next day. If a simple routine such as cleaning the plates immediately after meals was in place, you will never arrive at the point when you have a filled up dishwasher. So, act fast in your attempt to get rid of clutter before it begins to accumulate.

Going by with less and getting rid of window shopping are also ways to keep track of clutter building up all over again. It has been suggested that you never purchase an item that is not on your shopping list. This way, you do not accumulate more than you need and end up with more possessions that you have no place to keep. This leaves no room for exceptions. Therefore, do not accumulate newer items even if it were on a promotional basis. When you see that buy one, get one free tag, ensure you buy it only because you need it.

To keep track of clutter, you must be open to receiving and asking for help. Use support systems like a timer or an additional hand to help you cut out clutter. Having someone work on the garage while you work in the kitchen could be a much needed relief.

When decluttering your computer, you can create a folder to drop files whose exact use you are not sure of at that moment. Keeping track of clutter is about controlling it in a way that it does not accumulate.

It is very easy and in fact convenient to acquire more items because our home is newly decluttered. We can very easily see the newly acquired space as an excuse to get newer items. However, this will only take us to where we were before we began considering decluttering.

Getting Rid of Sentimental Clutter

This is the most difficult task when it comes to getting organized. Sentimental clutter is a result of holding on to sentimental items even though they have lost significance for us. Sentimental items are different from person to person but they are objects in our home that we have given meaning to. We find it hard to let go of items that we have attached feelings to or that hold special memories for us.

Aside other disadvantages, holding on to items we do not need only prevent us from creating newer memories with other items. By getting rid of possessions we do not need or truly want, we are able to enjoy the things we do need.

These objects represent people, moments and experiences for us and as a result, we find it hard to let them go. Although, it's hard to let these things go, getting rid of the clutter they create is an essential part of our home organization endeavors. Here are a few tactics to help you get rid of sentimental clutter.

1. Give yourself a deadline

Before you begin taking out sentimental clutter, designate a time frame within which you can hold on to them. This way you can enjoy looking at your special items for one or two last moments. Setting a specific time within which to declutter these items will keep you from procrastinating and postponing the D-day.

2. Invite Your Loved Ones

In order to avoid getting really emotional, have your best friend or someone you trust come around to help you declutter. They can help keep you accountable and from refraining to set the sentimental items aside. You might even get lucky enough to have someone who wants the items you intend to put away.

3. Evaluate the items again

As you pick each item, try to evaluate how much value they still hold in your life. Ask yourself if you would buy the item all over again and if the memories it gives you are happy ones. Separate the people from the items. There may be significant moments and people you have attached to the item that makes you hold on to it. Learn to separate these people and happy times from the objects by telling yourself that it is the item you are letting go of and not the person or moment in question. You can consider re-gifting gifts or otherwise shutting out the guilt that comes with giving them away. You can also give the objects out as donations.

4. Declutter again

If after letting go, you still have a lot of your sentimental items hanging around your house, then you need to take another look. Go through the process again aiming to reduce the items as much as possible. You can also digitize them if you are finding it hard to get rid of them. Things like photos and videos are easy to digitize. Consider how these items align to your greater purpose before you hold on to them indefinitely.

5. Begin using the remainder

The items that are left after you get rid of sentimental clutter should not be hidden away in cabinets. They should be given special places in your home because they were valuable enough to withstand decluttering. Experts have suggested that this action can help ease the guilt that decluttering sentimental items carry.

MAKING ORGANIZING AN EASY HABIT

One of the easiest ways to keep track of clutter is to make organizing an easy habit. You must make your organizing as easy as possible. Set up a routine that makes you shuffle between your decluttering with ease. This is more or less getting ahead of clutter for the long term. You do not want a relapse and you do not want your home to look anything like what you used to have before you began organizing. You do not want to return to that state ever again. To make organizing easy for you to do while turning it into a habit, you must carve out strategies to support this. We have done so for you and we will now outline how easy organizing can get below.

1. Use automation

Granted, some of our tasks will be urgent and important while others can wait. Some of them will also be repetitive in nature making it seem like you are engaged in a monotonous activity. To make this easy to deal with, you must use tools that help you automate the tasks and allocate them to an assistant so that they no longer need your direct effort. You will find a host of automating services on the Internet.

2. Review at regular intervals

Set intervals for reviewing your organizational relapse. This could be monthly, weekly or quarterly, etc. For example, check your closet every month to see if there are clothes that you no longer need and declutter these accordingly. You can also check your storage areas for anything stored away that is only clogging your home.

3. Check for those stray files again

Each day, get rid of files on your computer that are only adding to clutter. These files can easily add up but constantly checking for them will give you an organized desktop.

4. Create boundaries

Set limits on your information consumption. Limit everything from how many hours you spend watching TV to how many people you follow on social media. Follow through on making use of the things you own before you obtain newer ones.

5. Set routines on recurring decisions

There are some minor decisions that we have to take everyday from what we eat for breakfast to what our kids will put on to school. Place a routine on these kinds of decisions so that you do not have to think about them every time. You can do this by deciding over routine matters well before they occur. For example, having a list of foods to eat for the entire week, rather than thinking about what to eat each morning, helps you follow what you have predetermined for that day. This can also help you where you are trying to stock your kitchen for example. You can fill it up according to the foods that you will need within the set period.

6. Engage team work

Assign roles to members of your family that aligns with your organizational goals. Make each person in your family responsible for specific tasks that are aimed towards combatting clutter. For example, one person can be responsible for dishwashing while the other is responsible for cleaning their bedroom. This way, everyone is involved and clutter becomes easier to tackle. It can even make the whole process fun in the end. Another way to use team work in organization is to involve friends. Invite your friends to help you organize and schedule times to go organizing their own homes thereby rotating the decluttering activity.

7. Adopt organizational tools

We have talked about organizational tools in the preceding chapter. Getting some of the tools or any other that best suits you will make organizing easy for you to handle. for example, bins, baskets and trays are indispensable, in attaining an organized home.

ESSENTIALISM

Essentialism is an organizational concept developed by Greg McKeown and projected through his book **Essentialism: The Disciplined Pursuit of Doing Less.** It is a concept positing that we should take on less tasks as opposed to the world's standards of doing more in order to achieve success. Essentialism has been defined as the art of discerning between external noise and internal voice. However, it is a mindset rather than a time management or task management set of rules.

Essentialism is predicated upon deviating from the societal crave for more work towards effectiveness with limited tasks. We live at a time when overworking is applauded. We seem to think that success is within the reach of the next task. So we take in more work and hope it will bring our big break.

However, it never is and we take things even further by trying to solve the problem with even more work. But is that really the case? Does our craving for more work and our actual participation in more work lead us to the success we envision? The answer is sadly no. Taking on more than we can do only leads us to a path of overwhelming stress.

Essentialists believe that there is a better way to do things and not all work must be carried out by you. Essentialism redirects our focus to the things that are more important in life which are our health, our family and our general wellbeing. The drive to do more is characterized by a popularization of career success and wealth over our physical and emotional wellbeing. So even if the extra work on our plate is causing us stress, we take it on anyway because we see it as one step towards our potential break financially and career wise. We never prioritize our lives. The reason why society has a culture of always adding on work is because we have become consumers. We always want more. We always want the next big gadget and so we try to work harder to be able to afford them. We also want to be the next big name and we think that working endlessly will help us attain that status. It rarely does. It only eats up and distorts our wellbeing. Greg puts it aptly when he said, "Our whole society has become consumed by the undisciplined pursuit of more.

The only way to overcome this problem is to

change the way we think - adopt the mindset of only doing the things that are essential - and do it now." Thus, we must develop an essentialist mindset. We must join the movement. We need to shift into the 'new way of thinking'.

To become an essentialist, you must be 'insanely selective'. You must explore new opportunities with the mindset of taking on only a certain amount of work that you can perform excellently without distorting your wellbeing. This is evidenced by the fact that a large number of people who currently practice essentialism paid so much for trying to do everything.

Essentialists believe that less means more and more equals mediocre. They train themselves and practice something called "tradeoff" through which they decline tasks that they cannot complete. They are honest about what tasks they trade off and are okay with communicating this to other people.

The principles of essentialism include:

1. Contemplation

Essentialists contemplate their actions rather than acting impulsively. They 'live by the delayed yes.' They make decisions based on their internal clarity of purpose rather than on external pressure. Delaying your response helps you determine if something is truly essential. You can practice how to become an essentialist. Take a moment to think before you say yes to the next task.

2. The Joy of Missing Out

Essentialists practice the joy of missing out and discard the fear of missing out. They know that a packed calendar is not necessarily useful and they do not have to take advantage of every opportunity. Rather, they take advantage of opportunities that are essential to their purpose. Pass on something you cannot handle and if this presents you with extra time then use the time to explore opportunities that are relevant to you and tasks that you can accomplish.

3. Anti-endowmentalist

The Endowment Effect says that we value

objects and opportunities higher if we own them than if we don't. Essentialism suggests that you do not have to own something in order for you to value it. To practice essentialism, you must be an anti-endowmentalist.

4. Add more time into your planning equation

Greg says, "Things inevitably take longer, doing fewer things and choosing more carefully is essential." When we set out to do something, we underestimate how long it will take us to accomplish it. This makes us to add more and more unto our plate rather than taking out of it. The result is the pressure of pending deadlines and the inability to complete tasks. Essentialism suggests that we stop making the fool's bargain.

5. Weigh your activities by their importance

This means that you should set priorities. The fact that you have so much to do or so much to take on does not mean that they are equally important. Deciding which tasks to choose among so many requires setting real priorities.

6. Work towards real results and not towards being popular

It is okay not to be at every function as long as these do not move you in the direction of your goals. Trying to be everywhere so that you get known is not essentialist in nature because what is important is your contribution and not your presence especially when this presence will only make you burn out.

7. Be present in the moment

Guard against activities that take you off the present moment throughout your day. Today's information world makes this all too easy. We can get carried away by our electronic devices and forget the things we should be doing. Turn off the distractions and get into the real world. Also, get in the moment by reducing 'the impulse to always have something to do.' It's okay to not be busy.

As an essentialist, you rearrange the unspoken hierarchy in society. Thus, the things you achieve such as career success and wealth are only important as they relate to your health, your wellbeing, the wellbeing of your family and your personal fulfilment. Learn how to say no without guilt. Recognize that pressure is not the same as purpose. Listen to your internal voice in decision making rather than the external pressure to do more. Essentialism helps you manage your time in such a way that your efforts within the limited time are directed towards achieving the things you truly want. Not the things everyone wants you to accomplish. This way you can enjoy the results of your efforts and feel like you truly own them.

CONCLUSION

A study has shown that viewers are often unable to interpret the expressions on the faces of television characters when the background on the screen is full of clutter. If this is true, it means that clutter can negatively impact our visual perception in the same manner that it does our brain's ability to process information. This is only one of the reasons that clutter isn't good for you. Along with the other disadvantages that we have already pointed out in this book, it is essential that we get rid of clutter.

The most effective way to deal with this

situation is to get organized. However, your home is not the only thing you have to organize. You have to deal with the clutter in your mind and the one in your brain, namely emotional clutter and mental clutter respectively in order to get your life organized as well and completely eliminate stress. When the stress is gone, you will be left with enough mental, emotional and physical space to induce productivity. What follows is effective results and bountiful joy. This is the crux of this book. This also is something that everyone should attain to.

When my husband and I walked into our living room one day to see broken toys piled on top of each other on our sofa, we knew instantly that it was time we considered organizing our home. I was so frustrated at the mess that my little ones had made of our living room and I was all the more embarrassed because we had been accompanied by Frank's colleague at work who was just visiting us for the first time. I had to hide my hysteria as I picked up the toys and made space for the visitor to sit. On that day, I knew that clutter in our home had gotten out of hand. So, I began my home organization with a clarity of purpose which was that I never wanted that scene to happen again. It seemed daunting at first. When Frank glanced at me, I knew he felt the same way.

How had we gotten such a messy house on our hands and where were we going to begin our home organization? Then, we learnt about decluttering and we incorporated it into our organizing strategy. As each room got cleaned up, we got a bit more excited. It was also amazing the things we saw hidden away at locations where we could never have found them. We found our son's pair of sneakers in the garage inside an abandoned bin. It was hilarious.

When we were done organizing the entire house, I realized what enormous stress we had been going through. I used to rush off to buy things I already had because I could not find them but today, that is not the case. Every drawer and cabinet in our house has specific items designated to them. As a result, I never have to look for anything anymore. I know exactly where to find them. We are all much happier now and life is less stressful than it used to be.

These principles of home organization have been outlined in this book. The book has also provided you a step-by-step guide to organizing your home as well as tips and steps for decluttering other aspects of your life. You can use it to answer your questions regarding how you should start your home organization and the details that fill-up the entire process and gets you to a successful end. After having read this book, you will come away from it with enough reasons to stop postponing your organizational

goals. We hope that this is the case for you.